Praise for
Marketing to Serve

How much did I love *Marketing to Serve*? Well, I read it all in one sitting (which almost never happens) and moments after beginning, ran to grab pen and paper so as not to miss any tidbits.

I totally related to the first few chapters and eagerly read for Cassie's solutions. I now have two pages of suggestions, and I contacted her to book a strategy call! I love the distinction between wanting to make money and **planning** to make money, as well as the idea of creating my vision for my ideal live prior to establishing a marketing plan. And **love** only having to pick one to three marketing methods. It feels so easy and do-able now!

I will definitely be re-reading this gem, as well as recommending it to every entrepreneur I know! Thanks for sharing Cassie!

ALEXANDRIA BARKER

Most marketing books and courses totally turn me off with their 'push' energy and their insistence that I have to fill every spare minute of my day with things I don't want to do. Cassie's book is different. She mixes vision, marketing and intuition...two of my favourite things with one of my business needs. In this equation, I can see me actually enjoying my marketing more and for the first time in nearly 12 years in business, I think I might actually create a marketing 'plan'. Thanks Cassie!

DONNA HIGTON

Wow! Just WOW! Cassie Park's new book, *Marketing to Serve* is refreshing, recharging and revitalizing! I never thought "marketing" could be so fun! Like most entrepreneurs, who only want to serve and make a difference, we struggle "trying so hard" to do it right, follow conventional practices or pushing ourselves to the point of exhaustion. Then we go into self-loathing and wondering how we thought we could ever do it in the first place and wanting to just throw in the towel and quit. We've all been there at one time or another.

This marketing book is unique. In *Marketing to Serve*, Cassie Parks not only described exactly what I had been thinking and feeling about my business, but the very reasons I felt that way! It was like she was reading my mind! But she didn't leave me there. *Marketing to Serve* gives you a complete marketing plan so you not only get to where you want in your business, but will restore your faith in yourself, your clients and what how you want to serve.

Marketing doesn't have to be so hard! In fact, it can be the most exhilarating and satisfying thing you've ever done, leading to a life and business that you love!

Five stars Cassie!!

MINDY J KALETA

There are so many suggested ways to market your business swirling about, that I would get overwhelmed and end up doing nothing except posting on my Facebook business page. In *Marketing to Serve*, author Cassie Parks invites you to give yourself permission to narrow it down to one to three ways of marketing your business, while inviting you to use your intuition to choose the avenues that speak to you the most. A wave of relief washed over me to hear her explain why this strategy works and how I can be successful without doing everything under the sun. I now feel confident in creating a marketing plan that works for me, and I feel inspired to move forward in serving my clients even more, as I am no longer paralyzed by overwhelm. Thank you, Cassie!

SUYIN NICHOLS

MARKETING TO SERVE

The Entrepreneur's Guide to Marketing
to Your Ideal Client and Making Money
with Heart and Authenticity

cassie parks

Table of Contents

CHAPTER 1

Confronting the Learning Curve

Jodi is so smart, and a fun person. She's always positive and optimistic, so everyone looks to her for advice. So it made perfect sense when she felt the calling—*to become a coach*. After all, she didn't love her corporate job. She's a hard worker, and maybe because of her work ethic and the pressure, the hours were longer and longer, and started to cut into too many of the things she wanted to be doing. When she found her heart called to coaching, and making a difference in other people's lives, it felt like the perfect move. She could make her own schedule, do what she loves and make money.

She'd heard all the positive sayings and encouragement from successful coaches: "Leap and the net will appear." "Do what you love and the money will come." And she believed them; it was as if no one had had any regrets or really tough experiences. It seemed like everyone she knew was more than able to navigate the adjustment to being on their own and doing what they loved. So, she made the leap!

Except now, Jodi is sitting anxiously in her office, staring at the familiar screen with a blue border. She's checked all her notifications. There was one in there from a client, but the rest were just notifications about people posting in the entrepreneurs' and coaches' groups that she's signed up for. Some are courses she's taken, and others are launchers' or accountability groups intended to provide sounding boards or positive energy.

It's probably time to prune down the notifications for groups again, but then what else would she get notifications for? Every time she sees 12 notifications since her last login, Jodi gets really excited. Maybe, just maybe there will be someone commenting today on one of her posts. Maybe they want to hire her, or they're at least looking for someone who does this work. Maybe just maybe there will be a client in there. Jodi has focused on social marketing because it seems like one doesn't need to have a lot of background to make it work.

She opens her news feed and scrolls through. Nothing as far as clients are concerned, but she sees a new six notifications for a group discussion, so she clicks in there. Wonderful, all six are from lovely people sharing how successful their latest launch was, how much money they made and noting it's only the sixth of the month, or checking in from another vacation because their business now runs itself. Lots of dreams coming true! Jodi just scans instead of reading, because if she reads all this awesomeness in one go, she might have to shove her pen through her eye.

Uggh! First the anger sets in. *Why can't I do that? Nothing I am doing is working. One of those girls offers something I don't even understand. The other one doesn't appear very smart, and the rest, well, I can't believe someone paid them for these programs.* Then the sharpness of the anger dissipates a little and she's left with a familiar stuck feeling, like a veritable roadblock of frustration. And then that sting distills further, and she's left with that sinking feeling in her stomach. Just to make sure she's right, she checks her Paypal account. Yep, the same $287.22 that was there at the end of last month, still there. She doesn't want to take it out because she's probably going to need it for something in her business. If she does transfer it to her bank account, she doesn't know how long it's going to be before something else shows up. Keeping it there dulls the pain a little because it feels like at least she's made some money.

Jodi feels like a failure. Unlike her chosen "peers," she's not a best-selling author, she didn't just have a $50,000 launch, and all that's booked on her calendar this week is that one dedicated client who's always been there, almost since she opened her door. She's not quite sure why, but this client loves her. Jodi has helped her immensely, but even she wonders why this woman hasn't discovered the "Queen of using two words like a magic wand" to make everything better. That snarky caption pops into Jodi's head as she sees a new post in the group about a coach who helped her client change her whole life, and make $20,000 in five minutes.

Jodi sits in agony, again, wondering, "Why isn't *my* business successful?" She's on the verge of tears, thinking about smashing her computer—and then she hits a job board to see what's out there. That is a short foray though, because Jodi is really sure she doesn't want another job.

This is a scene that plays out at least once a week and has for months. What Jodi really wants, what her soul is longing for, is know-how about making a business work. She doesn't have to have a $50,000 launch. She'd be ecstatic to make a new $500 this week. Is that too much to ask of herself? "Aren't I a good enough coach?" she wonders. "I am smart. Sure I didn't get a marketing degree or anything to do with business for that matter, but I am smart. I know that. So why can't I figure this out?"

Jodi feels like she's tried it all. Seriously, if you opened her downloads folder, there are at least 10 $97 products in there about how to market your business. Some of the courses taught methods that didn't resonate. Some of them told her what to do, but there was no backup on how, and Jodi has yet to find the way to figure it out on her own. And there's even Jodi's own product. She was so proud when she created it, but found she could only sell two of them. She's been assuming the first sale was a fluke, and the second an accident.

Jodi has tried so many things before. She has spent so much money on trying to figure out how to get clients and make money alone. All those programs, now sitting idle on her computer, had plenty of testimonials of people who weren't making any money—and now since taking this course, their business is making more than enough. "Why isn't that me? Why didn't it work for me? Seriously—is there something majorly wrong with me?"

Jodi closes the computer and sits there, knowing that if she's too hard on herself it will never work. She takes a deep breath and thinks about it *working*, picturing herself making enough money to go get a massage and relax. She hasn't treated herself in ages.

Jodi has been working so hard, but that hard work is not working. She is miserable. She never shows that on the outside, of course. When someone asks about her business, she says something like, "It's growing," or, "This is going to be a good month." She has gotten those answers down to a science, because she doesn't want to be unconvincing to anyone's confidence in her, let alone let on the full reality that she has no idea how to fix it. She actually skipped a party she had wanted to go to just last week, and only because she didn't want to answer the question about how her business is going. "Should I give this up? Have I tried everything?" She's not sure, but she *does* know she would do anything if she knew it was going to work. There is a constant ache in her stomach, it's a longing to be directed to what will work.

What will work? How can she create a business that not only pays her bills, but gives her free time and financial freedom to travel? *My goodness!* Jodi longs to see the ocean right now, to sit with the sand between her toes, smelling the salt, listening to the crash of the waves and the caws of the seagulls ahead. She just wants to walk out there, lay down on a beach in the salt air and soak up the warm of the sun. She longs to lay reading a book for fun, instead of trying to figure out what to do next for the business.

Jodi knows her work is amazing, too. When she actually gets a client, she knocks it out of the park. They experience amazing results. She is a rock star coach, she just don't have a rock star marketing plan...yet.

The reason Jodi isn't making money, experiencing success, or loving her business—yet—is because she never had a clear vision of what she wanted her life to look like when she stepped out of her job and into being a coach in the first place. Yes, she knew didn't want to work so many hours. She knew she wanted to make money, and she knew she wanted to help people. However, she had no clear picture of how all those puzzle pieces would fit together, or more appropriately, how she wanted them to fit together.

When the whole picture is clear, you'll be amazed at how easy it is to market, sell and serve clients. Your business is fun when it's working. It's easier to run when you are making money. As Jodi's coach, the first thing we're going to do is gather every single detail that she wants in her life. We're going to get her in touch with the complete experience she desires in her business, and more importantly, her whole life.

This is what I learned that made all the difference in my business...

My story isn't exactly like Jodi's, but I get it. I have been there. For years, I desperately tried to make my business successful. I tried and tried and tried, thinking more effort was the answer. I spent thousands—and I mean thousands of dollars—trying to make my business successful. It never was. I thought the answer was to get out of my corporate job early so I'd have the time to commit to my business I was pouring money at it, and that wasn't working, so I thought pouring more *time* into it was the right answer.

Between 2009 and 2012, I invested over $16,000 in marketing and trying to market my fledgling business. Between those years, I got one coaching client, (who spent a total of $800), sold one program ($47), and a few products ($90). I am a smart woman, so why did I keep doing this? Because I wanted my business to work, and I just didn't know how to do it. I hired a social media consultant because I thought that would be the ticket to making my sales work. She actually helped me create a video series for sale as a self-study product, as well. The only video that series sold was the first one that my social media person bought because she wanted to get the ball rolling and have me feel what a sale felt like. I hired an SEO specialist because I thought if my website had better SEO then I would sell stuff. I want to a conference where the guy assured me I would have 10 clients before dinner on the first night. Yeah, that was my bad to believe that hype. I invested $7500 in that experience. I had a podcast on an internet radio network. Oh and then there's the worst marketing plan I ever had, which I'll tell you about later.

Seriously, I should have figured this out sooner, but I couldn't because I didn't yet know what I didn't know. More importantly, I didn't know what I *needed* to know. There was no way I could have made it work without knowing what I needed to know, isn't that a wonderful paradox?

I forgave myself for all those missteps a long time ago. The first thing I would suggest you do is forgive yourself for your efforts that haven't panned out, and for the judgment you've imposed on yourself. Until this moment when you picked up this book, you haven't known what you didn't know, and you couldn't know what you needed to know. It's ok—all the mistakes you think you have made, all the money you feel like you have wasted in the process. Forgive yourself for all of that. Seriously, take a few moments now to connect to forgiveness and relief—or put it on your calendar to do it once you finish the book. It's that important.

Forgiving yourself for all the things you think you have done wrong and the mistakes you think you made is the very thing that opens the space to create something new. It's harder to create a new path when you're carrying old baggage around. If you want to do it differently from here on out, forgive yourself for all that stuff in the past. Especially, the courses you bought thinking they were the answer and didn't do the work to start. In fact, I would get rid of them literally, digitally, and physically, too. Start this part of your journey clean. Let's leave all that stuff in the past, so you can move forward light and open. If you aren't sure how to forgive yourself, you can get my forgiveness ritual process by going here http://www.liveyourchampagnelife.com/marketing-tool-kit/

You can't change what has been done—or not—in the past. In the end, the things that didn't work out or that you can clearly see in hindsight didn't make sense will become fuel and resonant credibility in the stories you tell about your path to success. It's how you learn, and how everyone else learns. My mentor says, "All marketing works." That is SO true, but we don't always choose the right strategies and tactics to fit our needs or our gifts, and that's where it falls down. If you implemented any of those strategies, and they didn't work for you, you now know they don't work for you and that is ok.

Hopefully you figured that out sooner than I did in many instances. My "worst marketing plan ever" is one of those stories that's kind of fun to tell now, but really wasn't funny at the time. It started out as a *good* plan. Right after I had done my Opening to Love weekend workshop with my housemates, I had performed a good test and was planning to start selling the workshop to new clients. There was a singles event, which I somehow found out about, at which they were selling table space for $75—the event was about three hours. I thought that was the perfect place to market it, and it was only $75. I was willing to invest that and a few hours to figure out if it was the right place. So, I said yes!

The night of the event rolled around. My really good friend agreed to go along with me. We took poster boards and made a simple poster that said, "Free hugs and kisses." Then we put out Hershey's hugs and kisses. *That* was actually genius marketing. We were creating awareness and drawing people in to our booth to learn more. I had 40 people sign up to take the free hour workshop teaser, and we had a lot of fun simply connecting with people and talking about what I did. It was a great night. The whole ride home, we both kept saying how much fun we had. And I had 40 new people for my list, which I thought was fantastic. I'd never gotten 40 new people in one day before. I felt amazing.

I added those 40 people to my contacts list. And then I sent them an email invitation to the free workshop. Two people showed up to the workshop, and one person signed up for the buy one get one free offer I made at the workshop for individual sessions. I made $125 to show for my $75 and 5 hour time investment. That isn't a great return on investment. In fact, that comes to a whopping $10 an hour. I was making much more than that at my job. I was happy though, because I felt like I had experienced *some* success.

If I had someone to point out that that plan really wasn't effective enough, I wouldn't have done what I did as my next step. I thought this was great for a first try. *The perfect way to get people to sessions with me is to connect with them at public venues*, I thought. So, I signed up to have booths open at all the major events in the Civic Center Park in Denver. This investment was much more. It was about $1000 to run booths at three key events. The time commitment was *way* more. I had to be present in the booth from 10—6 each day for 2—3 days, depending on the event. I was excited about the first one. I invested in new signs that I ordered online. Once I got there, I realized I wasn't really prepared for events on this level at all. A tent, a table and a sign didn't compare to the elaborate set ups the "professionals" had. I felt out of my league.

It also turns out that people at those kinds of community events aren't as into stopping at a booth and talking about life coaching at all. At the first one, I didn't sell any books, nor did I get any clients. That was a 0% rate of return. To top it off, I was still working that full time job at the time, which meant I gave up my entire weekend off manning my little booth at this event. That meant I was exhausted, in addition to frustrated. The whole process was tiring. Lugging everything in from the car into the park. Taking everything back to the car. Sitting out in the sun all day. It was miserable, and I still had two more events I had committed to do!

Looking back at that point, I should have just considered the money lost and backed out of the other events so that I regained my free time. By the end of the summer, I had given up four weekends, spent well over $1000, and gained zero new clients. I was frustrated and felt dumb for thinking this little plan would work. I was sad, too, because I could have taken four weekend vacations with the time and money I had invested in it. I could have gone to LA and the beach *four times!* Instead, I had invested my time and money yet again in my business and I felt no closer to experiencing success. On top of those feelings of defeat, I was exhausted because I spent all my time off trying to make my business work so I could leave my job.

I really believed you just had to keep doing things and persevere and you would succeed. Back then, I believed if you simply worked hard enough you would eventually be successful. The thing is, working hard won't always get you what you want. You have to work *smart*. You have to have a plan and you have to know how to evaluate that plan to know if it will work well. You have to know some things that you probably don't yet know, and that is how to evaluate a marketing plan and how to optimize it if it's working, or tweak it if it isn't.

While it was fun and felt good, having a table at the singles event really didn't work all that well. It worked a little, so I could have optimized it. Or I could have taken a small step, like registered for one more event in the park, and tested to see if I could optimize and make it more profitable than the singles event had been. Diving in deep, because I thought I had figured out the secret to my success—when I didn't have the numbers to back it up—was a huge mistake. *But all marketing works.* I now know *not* to market my business at park events in Denver. Some lessons we learn the really hard way.

If you work hard without working smart you will end up broke and exhausted, too. I don't want that for you. I know you are amazing, and someone—lots of them, perhaps—in the world needs your special skill and your experience. They are only waiting for you to figure out how to reach them. They want to pay you money to solve their problem, and help them make their life better. It's already in their wallet. They're waiting, desperately, to hand it over to the right person at the right time. They can't see you yet, because you don't know how to market *to them*.

I want you to experience a day like I did recently, where in the first 9 days of the month, your income is fully 21 times what it was the same month of the previous year. I want you to get paid for your genius and to be able to do it joyfully. I want you to experience the successful, amazing business you have been dreaming of for so long.

You are worth living that dream.

CHAPTER 2

Let's Go Swimming In Bora Bora

Do you have a picture on your vision board of huts in Bora Bora? The ones that are placed in the ocean, surrounded by the clearest most beautiful blue, green water? You know the place I'm talking about. These are often marketed as vacation spots, where your small house or "cabin" hut is built into the tide, surrounded by the most beautiful clear water. Even if it's not on your vision board, you have probably visualized it at least once before, because so many people want to go there. People are attracted to that place. Why? It's simple—people are attracted to clarity. People love to be able to see what's happening all around them, and to be able to see the big picture, and through to the details behind the impression.

Clarity is very attractive, whether it's rendered in a blue-green ocean or into a person on a mission. We're drawn to people who we feel like know where they are going. We're attracted to people who offer a strong sense of where they're going. We're attracted to people who can give us clear answers. Clarity is very, very attractive.

In marketing, there are words and pictures used, and then there is the energy or intention behind them. You have probably looked at something before and thought, *I should like that*, or, *I should want that*, but for some reason it just felt off. Something wasn't clear, either in what you could see, or perhaps the lack of clarity was felt behind the scenes, by the person who designed or produced the ad, in the agency.

The key to marketing is to be as attractive as possible *to your ideal clients*. So often, service based entrepreneurs think that in order to have attractive marketing, or successful marketing, they have to do something that doesn't feel good to them, and they get an icky feeling around sales and marketing. That is actually not true! In fact, if you're unsure and unclear, the marketing is going to turn out unsure and unclear, no matter what you do.

Jodi's clients and customers aren't showing up right now because she is not clear on a number of things. She is not as attractive as she could be to her clients, because she is not clear about the money she wants to make, nor who she wants to serve, how she wants to serve them, even most importantly, about where she is headed (as in, her dream life, her happy ever after). Can you relate?

Why do people with a servant's heart like Jodi's avoid getting clear about the life of their own dreams? Here are some really common reasons, as I have gleaned through my coaching. The first one is they think some how dreaming big for themselves is selfish, and worse, isn't of service to their clients. That isn't true. Being really clear about your dream life allows you to serve as a lighthouse so that your clients can find you in the dark. It is a disservice to them *not* to get clear about your own vision and where you are headed. How often do *you* follow someone who has no idea where they are going? Even if you find them appealing initially, I suspect you don't stay in that circle for very long. Lack of clarity is not inspiring, and in fact the anxiety about not knowing where you are going is fairly contagious.

You can't serve, unless people show up to be served. And they can't *find* you to show up when there is no lighthouse beam. The best thing you can do to be a servant to your people is to get clear about your happy ever after—and start stepping into it.

Another common reason people with huge, servants' hearts don't create the vision of their dream life is that they think they are supposed to help everybody, and that they are required to put all their energy into helping. You are kind and generous, and you want to have a positive impact on the world. That desire to help "everybody" is keeping you from actually serving anybody. It's impossible to serve everyone...and quite honestly, not everyone has the unique set of challenges that you are best suited to help.

One truth that may bring some relief to this conundrum: if you serve who you are meant to serve, in turn *they* can go out and serve, in whatever capacity, who they are meant to serve. Trying to serve everyone will end up serving no one. Let go and trust that there are enough servants in the world that everyone who wants to be helped will receive the support they want and need. You do not have to do it all on your own. It is not your world to save.

I'm guessing you are good at more than one thing. Those with servants' hearts usually are. Being good at more than one thing can also keep you from getting clear on your big why, because you're afraid your "other" talents will go to waste. They will never go to waste, really, because you can often use all your talents to serve your clients. Getting clarity and picking a path won't keep you from cultivating your talents. Instead, it will open up opportunities to use *all* of your talents because you will have more clients to serve, more confidence in your business, and more free time to develop yourself.

In the same way you're afraid some of your talents might go to waste, you're afraid that by getting clear and picking a single way to serve that you'll be missing out on opportunities that could be just as exciting, but come through doing something else. This is common. You want to enjoy what you do and you're afraid if you pick just one thing you won't get to do anything else. I'll show you, later in the book, how you can actually do it all.

What I have seen as the most *common* reason that entrepreneurs with a servant's heart don't get clear about themselves is because they *don't know how*. There is a lot of material out there that will tell you how to market, how to make money, how to grow your business, but a lot of times it doesn't *feel good*. You haven't found the *feel good* way to market your business—you guessed it—because you don't yet know how to get clear about your vision.

You resist because you don't want to feel sleazy and slimy. You want to serve from your heart, while still being able to afford to eat dinner and buy new shoes. You want to love what you do, honor those you serve and make money, but they didn't offer that class in college, or if they did, you were interested in something else. All this time, when you were buying $97 products and taking free webinars, you were looking for that *exact* class, but you didn't find it. The good news is, the answer you have been looking for is in this book and it is this book that will actually show you *how* to do the one thing that matters—get clear about what your dream life looks like and then follow the path. That is the key to marketing.

Getting clear about your dream life isn't what you have been taught. You might have heard you need to set a big goal. Having a clear vision of your dream life is different than a big, overarching goal. A goal might be just one number on a piece of paper, or a level of attainment in the form of a title. It's *a thing*. It might even be a little scary to contemplate. That isn't all bad, and most people will tell you that if it doesn't scare you a little it isn't worthwhile. A goal is good, but it gets a lot more power when supported by a vision. A vision is a detailed, textured, complex taste of your life ahead, and feels really good to explore. Your vision is a clear, fun, juicy destination you are headed too.

Stephen Covey says, "Begin with the end in mind." The vision of your dream life is the end. Where are you going? The life you have been dreaming of is, and should be, more than just a number on a spreadsheet or a list of achievements.

Being clear about where you are headed helps guide you. Guidance and clarity give you confidence, and a way of engaging in the world that makes you more attractive to your potential clients, even if they don't know the big vision you have. They can sense it and feel that you have one. When someone invests in you, they want to know you are going to be around for them until they end their engagement. Having clarity in your own long term vision and destination gives people that sense that you are going to be a long term partner for theirs, assuming you are a fit now.

Some people will swim in swamps, but most people don't like it—think about it, not being able to see if there an alligator looming or not. On the other hand, people will take their "trip of a lifetime" to Bora Bora to experience that clear water all around them. Let's look at the worst marketing plan ever in terms of clarity. To sum it up, *there was none*. I had no idea who I was serving. I had no idea how many clients I wanted. I had no idea how much time I had to give or wanted to give, and I didn't even know how much money I wanted to make.

My waters were muddy as can be, and yet I was hoping people would jump in with me. Think about standing on the bank of a swamp, with your best friend trying to convince you to jump in. How much talking does your friend have to do to get you to jump in? How much do you have to trust them? Could your best friend realistically convince you? What about a total stranger? I'm guessing you wouldn't even consider jumping in if it was a total stranger trying to convince you that swimming in that muddy swamp will turn out fine—let alone change your life for the better.

Now, turn it around. Imagine you are trying to convince someone you don't really know to jump into the muddy swamp with you. Imagine being there—you can't see the bottom. You've been told that there are no alligators, but you don't really know, and certainly can't confirm that for yourself now. How much energy is it going to take to convince that new person to jump in the swamp with you? Is it going to be energizing or exhausting to do? Feel into that scene. What do you think about? How does it make you feel? Empowered or desperate?

Now imagine you are standing waist deep in the crystal clear blue green ocean waters of Bora Bora, calling someone else in to join you. Do you think you would have to yell more than once, or convince them once you got their attention? Is it possible they would just come in and join you before you even asked? Thinking about that scenario, would it be easy or draining?

Getting someone into the clear water would be easy, right? In fact, like I mentioned above, they just might decide to join you before they are even asked. That's the equivalent of someone just *finding you* to work with you. I have a client in my year-long program who has no idea how she initially found me, which means the attraction was so great she was just led to me by her own guidance. It wasn't a credit to my elaborate marketing plan. It was my clarity that allowed that ease and that magnetism. Would you rather invite people into the swamp or the ocean in Bora Bora all day? What have you been doing in your business?

Having my ideal client just "find" me, as opposed to the experience I had sitting outside for three days hoping someone would realize they needed me, feels completely different. The worst marketing plan was physically, emotionally and mentally draining. In fact, at the end of one of the weekends, a woman did approach and ask, "Oh is this life coaching?" I'm a little embarrassed to admit this, but I was so defeated and tired by then, that I just said yes and kept on packing up, rather than even engaging with her. In that moment, I wasn't serving myself and I was definitely not serving my potential client. The best way to serve yourself and your client is to get clear so you sustain the energy to serve them.

When I quit my job to become a full time coach, I really didn't know how I was going to make money. I figured I'd start taking on some one-on-one clients, which if I'm honest, didn't thrill me. I hadn't been successful marketing my business on the side yet, but I thought once I had more time, I'd surely figure it out. Remember, prior to quitting my job, I had sold some individual coaching, one program and less than ten $9 products. The good news is, for me, eating didn't depend on my making money through coaching. I had already built a real estate business that could get my basic bills paid while I built my coaching practice. Having fun depended on it, as the real estate income wasn't yet built for frills or growth, but because of my real estate income I'd always have security on life's essentials.

Four months after I quit my day job, I launched my first successful program. I called it Money, Money, Money. This launch proved (to myself as much as anyone) that I could do what I loved, serve my clients and make money in a way that felt really good to me. At that time, my biggest dream in terms of coaching was to launch a successful group program. I had achieved my dream of quitting my job, so although I wasn't solid in a big vision yet, but I did have a vision of success, and that experience allowed me to create that successful program.

Before I started writing that course, I was really clear about essentials and some specific details that fueled that program. For instance, who I would be serving, knowing I wanted to serve 170 of them, that I wanted to make money, and how much effort and time I wanted to put into working on it. I still didn't know how to market that course.

I enrolled people into that program from a blog post, not a fancy sales page, and realized after 50 people had signed up that I didn't even have the dates for the program on the post. Clarity is attractive—absent communicating the specifics, I was clear about the outcomes I wanted and how I wanted to experience them. This program was a "pay after you manifest," and I made $6800 from it the first time through. Clarity is attractive, and when you are clear, most marketing "rules" don't need to apply.

I scripted the outcome I wanted to experience from that course. I knew the experience I wanted to have, and I knew it inside and out. That deep connection to that future place, that clarity of what I wanted to experience in vivid detail is what made that course attractive.

I marketed that course by intuition alone. I didn't really know how to market, strategically or tactically speaking, or what to do to achieve a target, so I just stayed tapped into the clear picture of the outcome I wanted and followed my intuition to make it happen. That intuition led to posting on Facebook at just the right times and people signed up and lots of people shared it. Over 200 signed up that way, in fact. Clarity is very attractive—the greater the clarity, the less marketing expertise required.

Money, Money, Money was successful, and even better, it felt energizing instead of draining. It took less energy and felt better to get 200 clients in that program than it did to get totally ignored like my previous launch had. The muddier your vision, the harder you have to work. The clearer you are about your outcomes and vision, the less effort it takes to be successful in your business.

Marketing Money, Money, Money was fun, but after a while it started to feel like work, and I wasn't getting as many people in as I wanted to each time. I found myself at a standstill, not knowing how to market it anymore. Why? Because I'd actually expired my vision. The clear vision that carried that course to success had already been fulfilled, and I hadn't created another one at all. So, marketing felt hard again, there was no ease, flow or inspiration. It was never as hard as the worst marketing plan ever, but it wasn't easy like I wanted it to be.

That summer, I had an idea to write my story called *Retired at 32*, with the intention people who read it would sign up for *Money, Money, Money*. I wrote it, edited it, and gave it away for free on my 33rd birthday. One hundred people downloaded it, but I don't think anyone signed up for *Money, Money, Money* after reading it.

This definitely wasn't back to the worst marketing plan ever, but it didn't really work. Why not? Because I didn't have a big vision. I wasn't clear about where I was going. The clear vision of a successful program was good enough for the first launch of Money, Money, Money, but it had happened, and there was nothing left to "come true". I had achieved the vision as desired, and basically I was walking around again with no vision, no clarity. I was muddy again. Back to trying to convenience people to jump into waters they can't see into.

I realized it was time to create a really big vision, my whole big dream life, so i went to work on that. I started gathering the details and creating the clear picture. I started thinking about what I wanted to experience in my dream life. That vision was all about what I wanted to *experience*. There was no mention of how many clients or what kind of work I was doing. It was all about how I wanted to feel, how I wanted my days to flow, and other experiences I wanted to have.

As that vision crystalized, I started to be drawn to Angela Lauria of the Difference Press (publisher of this book). I listened to the nudges and I got on the phone with her. We talked about my business. By the end of the call, I knew

I had to write a book with her. That conversation took place on a Friday, and I started writing *Money Mindset for a Champagne Life* the following Monday.

The marketing plan found me, because I was clear. I didn't "think" I should write a book, or go figure out how or think about whether I should print *Retired at 32,* and that is because my dream vision was clear. I knew where I was going and therefore the path appeared.

A little more than a year after that conversation, I'm writing my fourth book (which you're reading) well on my way to the life I created in my vision. Next year, Difference Press is going to highlight me for one month. They are doing all kinds of PR and promotions with me to support my books, my movement and my vision. When you're clear the marketing *finds you,* and making money becomes easier.

I created the vision of the next version of my dream life and I continue to step into it every day. When I have a question about whether to market left or market right, I first connect with that vision with the person I am inside that vision, my future self, and the answer becomes crystal clear. It's intuitive, but it's also substantiated by the notion that a very targeted message to a very clear seeker will be more successful than watered-down generic anything. That targeted message comes straight out of my future vision.

We are taught that the offers we create, the words we use, and the places where we engage and market are the most important factors in success. That's not true. It does not matter what you are marketing when your ideal clients are not attracted to what you are selling. You are serving people, not just selling some trendy latest and greatest gadget. Traditional marketing works when you are just marketing a "thing," but when you are marketing something deeper, you need a deeper resonant marketing method.

Your business is tied to *you*, and naturally, this makes it much more personal. When a major brand markets a product or program, they don't worry about how it makes them feel. If sales drop because of the plan they came up with, they don't feel bad about themselves. They do not think about the campaign as a reflection of themselves. They may feel a sense of failure momentarily, but they look at the data again, make a new strategic decision or even shift to a new primary channel. They don't call themselves a failure.

You can't market like a big corporation, just selling, because that is not who you are and that is not what you do. Your ideal clients are attracted to you as a person and provider. Your energy, your presence, your dreams are all a part of what draws them in—just as they could buy products or services from a corporation, and might want to know more about the company's values, vision, and behavior. Except a big company has more diffused energy around its people—founders, leaders and employees all contribute. With an entrepreneur, especially a heart-centered service provider, it really does all depend on you. It's the strong pull of your focused energy on where you are going that will keep that needy, graspy, energy—stuff that repels the seeker—out of your marketing.

The reason you are grasping for clients is because you are grasping at your dream yourself. You have not spent the time to get clear about where you want to be going. And yet, something inside you is craving exactly that. Something inside your soul is craving to know most of all where you are going. Your *desires* are longing to be heard. Your soul is grasping at the pieces of your future it is longing for. In turn, you are grasping for clients. Once you satisfy the part of your soul that is longing for vision, and you know where you are going, the graspiness will become a distant memory.

You are likely trying to appeal to everyone, too, like a big brand. You can't do that. You're not a chocolate shop. You can't make fifty different yummy treats for every taste, and also offer gummy bears in every flavor so that everyone who walks through your door can find something that they are looking for. You have to figure out what it is you do best and most joyfully, so that the people who are looking for you walk through your door easily because they can find your beacon of light. Figuring out who you serve starts with getting clear about *your* dreams and where you are going personally.

It is so counterintuitive to think that marketing starts with getting clear about what *you* want but it does. We are taught to think first about our customers and clients and what *they* want. When you are actually serving others, you *must* serve yourself first. That is how you fill yourself up. It's how you begin to serve from *your overflow* so that there is always enough. Getting clear about your dream life is the best actual way to start a marketing plan.

Think of a coach or mentor you have followed, whether paid or unpaid. Why did you follow them? Was it what they were offering? What they were good at? Or was it more subtle, like their energy? What attracted you most to her in the first place? Like you, your clients are attracted to that feeling, that energy that you exude—and not necessarily focused solely on what you are selling. They will want to invest in what you offer once they are attracted to your energy. Your energy is your greatest marketing asset.

When you are crystal clear the path will reveal itself. Clients might just appear like the "ideal" client who signed up in my year-long program as I mentioned. You might get on a path to have an opportunity arise for someone else to promote you for an entire month. It might take the form of one Facebook post that gets shared a hundred times, or a thousand. Maybe a timely and perfect interview on a podcast leads to all the clients you're looking for. Get clear, and when you are, you will recognize opportunities that make a great fit, and it will even seem effortless to follow as it unfolds.

CHAPTER 3
Plan on Making Money

Looking back on all those long, hot hours in the park a couple of years ago, it's clear to me that I was *hoping* to make money instead of *planning* to make money. These are distinct differences between the two, and the outcomes you'll get from each one are distinctly different. One is muddy and one is clear. When you have a muddy start, you get a muddy outcome, and when you have a clear start, you get a clear outcome.

Before I registered for the singles' event, I was "hoping" to make money in my business. I spent years, actually, "hoping" to make money in my business. I definitely wasn't planning on it, or I wouldn't have been so willing to let go of $1000 when there really was no path to a return on that investment. I also didn't have a vision for my success, or why I was planning to earn that money.

You know when you're starving, let's say out with another person, and you have to decide where to go to dinner? In my experience, the waters start out pretty muddy in this scenario. Each person is "hoping" that the magical place they want to go out to eat will pop up in the discussion. One person throws out three suggestions, and the other person vetoes all of them. This pattern continues until the "hanger" sets in—you know, the hungry irritability that looks like anger—so you pick the closest, easiest place to get into the fastest. Usually, that's not the best meal of your life. It started out muddy, and it ends muddy.

If you are out and about, knowing what you want and need before it's urgent or desperate, and plan to be satisfied with your dinner, you have a plan to get that. In this case, you might make the three suggestions you desire. The other person picks one, too, and dinner is wonderful. When you go in planning to experience a good meal, you get a different outcome than you do when you're merely *hoping* to have a good meal.

This scenario happens all the time with entrepreneurs. You start your business because you are passionate. That passion doesn't automatically come with depth of knowledge comparable to a marketing degree. You have to figure things out along the way. You start out with big dreams of money, just pouring in. When that doesn't happen right away, you start trying everything under the sun to make something work. Just like when someone just starts throwing out restaurants.

In the restaurant scenario, the more hangry you become, the more ludicrous the choices become. The more frustrated you get, you also definitely get a lot hungrier. The same happens in business. The more tactics don't work, the more tactics you start frantically trying. You are hungry for success, and getting a little hangry and irrational. Sometimes, like in the worst marketing plan ever, you start trying some ludicrous things because you want to feel better.

Hoping to make money instead of planning to make money leaves you exhausted, broke and likely starting to question your abilities and resenting your business. That leads to more of the same, shame spirals and negative patterns, like sitting in front of Facebook watching people with $50,000 launches, comparing, despairing, and judging yourself.

I'm guessing you are following me by now, and can relate a little or a lot. So, how do you get clear about making money? For starters you have to get clear about the money and everything else. Here's how this usually goes. You get clear about the amount of money you want to make, or you get clear about the number of something you want to sell, clients you want to have, etc. For example, you decide one day, I want to make $5,000 a month in my business. Awesome. Is your business set up to do that? If you can't easily map out how $5,000 can come in, it's not set up to do that, so there's your action plan.

Here's another example, you say I want 5 clients a day. Cool, except that you also have in the back of your head that you only want to work a total of 5 hours a day. When are you going to market or do the other things that need to be done in your business?

The second common scenario happened with my client, Jessica. The first step in creating a successful business and life, of course, is to get clear on what that life looks like.

I started there with Jessica. We talked about how many clients she wanted, how much money she wanted to be making, how much free time she wanted to have, all of it. It was all great, but then I pointed out to her that the life she wanted didn't actually fit together as pieces of the same puzzle. There were contradictions. She wanted to work with corporate clients. She wanted 5 of them and she would work with them for about 5 hours a day. The problem was when we talked about the hours she wanted to be working, she only wanted to be working with clients 4 hours a day.

With Jessica I pointed this out to her. She realized she didn't want the structure that she thought she wanted, and adjusted her ideal down to 4 clients that fit into the amount of hours she wanted to be coaching. In her case, the time was more important than the money. Have you done something similar before? The original plan she had in her head was set up hoping to make money. Planning to make money means you are clear about how the pieces fit together.

It doesn't matter how good your marketing is, if something is amiss in the plan, the marketing won't land, because it can't. You can't attract something that you don't want. You would think the Universe would say, "Oh, I think she really only wants 4 clients so we'll just send those right over." It doesn't. It stays in a sort of paralyzing conflict and sends nothing over.

Have you ever sent someone to the store and told them to buy a specific brand of crackers, only they discover when they get to the store they don't sell that brand? The person stands there surrounded by crackers, wondering what the right choice is now, because it's not clear anymore. You gave clear instructions, but those instructions aren't possible to follow. The person doesn't make a decision, at least postpones it until they call you to review the plan. The Universe doesn't communicate like that. It communicates by sending you nothing, because it can't give you what you said you wanted, it won't work out.

You can only receive what you desire, in direct proportion to how clear you are about it. Have you ever said, "I want as many people as possible to buy this product," while simultaneously wanting, say $5000.00 in income. If the product is $97, then what you really want is clear—for 50 people to invest in it. If the product is $1997, you want 3 people to invest in it, and you're going to get more than you are asking for. Saying you want as many people as possible, while saying you want to make $5000, makes for a muddy message. It gets muddy results, or worse, no results at all. The pieces don't match. The picture isn't clear, so very little or nothing at all comes together.

When the pieces don't fit together, it's nearly impossible to create what you want, and you have to work really hard to get it. In order to experience success in the easiest and quickest way possible, you have to have the clearest vision possible. You have to be clear about what you're doing, who you're serving, even how many hours you want to be working. Then there is the most important thing to be clear about—and that is the life you want to be living while delivering your magic.

Who Are You Serving?

What does it look like to be clear about the people you serve? You have probably heard of an ideal client profile, a client avatar or your perfect customer. All of these are different ways of articulating the same thing. A clear picture and understanding of ideal person you are serving. The reason for creating one is so that you know who you are talking to in your marketing material. I really never understood this practice until about a year ago, which is why it doesn't surprise me that my experience with marketing was horrible up to that point.

One of the reasons the "worst marketing plan ever" was my worst plan had to do with not articulating who my ideal client was. I also had no idea if that ideal client would be realistically attending an event in the park. I didn't do it intentionally, but I did a good job of this when I did the singles' event. Odds are, my ideal people for the Opening to Love workshop were at the singles event. They probably were at the events in the park too, but I thought I wanted "everybody" to work with me so I was trying to market to "everybody." Quite literally everyone passed me by, because they didn't know who I was talking to, or didn't recognize it was aimed at them, specifically anyway.

I struggled for years trying to identify my ideal client, because at the time with the technique I was using, I *could* serve anyone. In fact, the clients I had at the time actually ranged in age from 14 to 65. They were comprised of both men and women. That's who showed up from referrals from people close to me. People always wanted me to choose a target demographic. I resisted.

I remember agonizing conversations where people, the ones who were meaning to help, felt like they were trapping me in a corner forcing me to make a decision I didn't want to make. The truth is, I couldn't make that decision for two reasons. The first was that I didn't know why it was important. To me, it felt like trapping myself and having to only work with one person and how did I know if I was going to like *that* forever? I had all those fears of missing out, and abandoning talents, and getting bored. Truthfully, the people trying to give me feedback didn't understand it either. They wanted to be helpful, and had heard enough times that you had to have a target market, so they kept trying to get me to define mine.

The real reason you focus your energy in this way is because when you speak to everyone, no one actually hears you. When you speak to your person, they hear you, and it actually opens up the space for everyone else to hear you, too. Imagine you are at a party, where everyone is having a conversation. If you tried to get *everyone* to hear you, you would have to shout. It would be hard to keep everyone's attention at once for very long. It would feel unnatural. People would stop listening, and go on about their own agendas. However, I'm sure you've experienced a moment where you are intimately engaged in a conversation with one person, and before you know it, the circle has grown to include 5-6 people, some participating, and some looking on hanging on your every word. This is why you choose an ideal client, and why you speak to them directly and intently, because when you are speaking to them intimately others are attracted into the conversation.

If I would have understood that, I don't think I would have felt as trapped by the concept, yet I still don't think I would have been totally on board with the idea. I still would have resisted picking, because just choosing *an* ideal client doesn't mean you'll pick the right one, at least not the first time. All those years, I think that was my own true fear and resistance to picking. What if I choose the wrong one? What if the other potential path was the reliable path to the money I wanted to make? What if I picked a client I thought I would like, but actually hated the experience of working with him or her?

I believe that resistance and fear shows up for good reason. I don't think you should just pick your ideal client. The ideal is more dynamic than that. You should be led to your ideal client by your future self, as she, the very one who is living the life you want to be living, also knows what kind of client is the right choice for taking you where you want to go.

If you pick your ideal client without being crystal clear, about the life you want to be living, you might not get to your ideal life as fast as possible. If you're serving clients, nothing is all that wrong. But if you feel a huge resistance to choosing an ideal client right now, it might be because you aren't yet clear on the future you want to be living.

How Are You Serving?

When you know who you are serving, you in turn have to decide how you are going be serving them. Again, this is a place that can cause deep turmoil when you're trying to figure it out. First, there are so many things out there that offer to tell you what to do to build your practice. You could write an ebook, or create a six-week program, you could create a product with five modules or a hundred modules, and the list goes on and on.

You're so knowledgeable that you have skills in a lot of areas, and seemingly lots of ways to apply what you teach. So you consider that you could offer 15 different products that cover everything under the sun. In the case of choosing *how* to serve, there are so many options that it can be so overwhelming and in that case you don't know what to choose. Sometimes that means not choosing anything as a practical matter, and staying stuck. Sometimes it means making a choice, but not being sure about it, because you are still hanging on to fears that you made the wrong choice.

Again, the fear of making the wrong choice, and the resistance to making a choice at all, is because your ideal life isn't clear. When you have a GPS point and you know where you are going, the path appears, although there isn't a crisp computer voice to tell you which way at every turn. The choices that do show up next, like, "How do I serve my people?" become clearer and easier to make. They feel natural and aligned instead of forced with effort. You feel drawn to them knowing they are right.

How Many Hours Are You Working?

How many hours do you want to be working in your business? Working doesn't just include client sessions themselves. It is also inclusive of your creative time, marketing time, answering emails, accounting, etc. One of the reasons you started your business was probably because you wanted to work less hours and have more freedom. Do you have that yet?

Your work schedule is a big piece of the puzzle to making money. If it doesn't feel good, you won't make as much money. If you're forcing yourself to work crazy hours, you won't make as much money. The key to making money easily is to feel really good about how you are making it and while you are making it.

So often, the decision of how much you want to work comes from external forces. It comes from stories, like the one that says you have to work a lot to make your business grow. This is a common perception. There are fears we pick up from cultural messages about work, too. If you don't work enough, you won't be taken seriously. And then there's the people that work all the time because they say they "love it," but again, just because you love what you do doesn't mean it has to be your *only* source of enjoyment. Work will take up as much time as you allow it. That's why it's important to get clear on what you want, and the life you want to be living.

The key to knowing the answers to the above, instead of guessing, is also knowing what the future life you want to be living looks like, inside and out. Knowing the details of how you want to experience your Happy Ever After is the key to making the right decisions, which will create the quickest and easiest path to get you there.

When you make decisions from the place of knowing where you are going, they aren't really decisions anymore. The answer becomes so clear, that you already know what to do. You automatically know who you are serving, how you are serving them, and what your work schedule looks like. You know what to do every day when you get up. With all those elements clear, you can't help but have a plan to make money. The plan practically creates itself. It's strong and based on intention rather than hope. That clarity makes your marketing plan easy.

A year ago, I set a big intention for my income, but then I let go of the income number and focused instead on the life I want to be living and every detail of how that will look. As I got clearer, my 2016 business plan evolved, and my new target is set 20% higher than I originally intended and I'm well on my way to achieving it. When you focus on the life you want to be living, the path gets created. What would it feel like to wake up and have *your* marketing decisions be clear and easy?

CHAPTER 4

Let Your Vision Lead the Way

Clarity is queen and she will create your queendom. When I was in high school, before I had a driver's license, my dad drove me to pick up a friend of mine. In high school, you aren't concerned with mundane details like addresses, so I didn't get hers beforehand. I'd been there once or twice, and accordingly I was sure I could find it. We drove around for quite awhile looking for her place once we got to her neighborhood. I would see a familiar turn and say, "Oh yeah, it's this street," only to realize at the end of that block that it wasn't.

In terms of directional metaphors, that story always stands out as the time I was the closest, but yet could not find my way to the destination I wanted. This was before the days of cell phones. And I couldn't page her without having a phone to get her address. So, there were two choices my dad had, and he was pretty patient about it. Drive me out of the neighborhood to a pay phone, or continue driving around with me, thinking I knew where I was going and would eventually pick up the cues from our surroundings. He chose to continue driving around. Eventually we found it and I did learn the efficient way to her house for the next time.

Today, that would be much less likely to happen as it did that night, because we have the magic of GPS in many cars and on our phones. If I was going to my friend's house today, and I wasn't sure I knew exactly how to get there, I would get the address and put in the GPS. *Voila*, directions to exactly the coordinates where I want to be.

Something magic happens when you put an address in the GPS. You expect to get where you are going. You know that once you put that destination in your GPS you are going to get there. Even if traffic is too busy and you can't get over fast enough to make the right hand turn you're being instructed to make by that crisp, bossy voice, you know you're going to get there. No matter which direction you take, your GPS is immediately going to recalculate the route and give you the quickest path to your destination from that new point.

The destination doesn't change once you put it in the GPS, which makes it a whole lot easier to get to, because the GPS zeroes in on it no matter what. It's rare that you change your mind, mid-route. You know for sure when you pick a destination you are going to get there, in spite of traffic, wrong turns or missed streets. You trust your GPS to get you where you want to go.

What is the GPS destination you've input for your business? If you are thinking the amount of money you want to make, or the clients who want to serve, good job. You have been paying attention. However, it's not either of those, nor is it the amount of hours you want to work. The GPS destination for your business is the coordinates of the complete life you want to be living. The whole picture of where you want to be, and how you want to be in your own life.

Most people *think* they know where they are going with their business. Or they think they will just see where they are going once they get around the corners. The result of that is the equivalent of my dad and I driving around looking for my friend's house. You get close, but you don't actually get what you want, because you do not *know* what you want, just like I didn't know the address. You get frustrated because you keep driving the same streets over and over again, or doing the same things over and over again while hoping for different results. You more or less wander aimlessly, hoping things will work out. That way is pretty frustrating and takes much longer than it needs to in order to create a successful business that you love.

Have you ever spent time thinking about whether you should do the next new action in your business? For example, there is a program that says it will give the results you want, but you're not sure about it. You get the ten emails talking about it. You almost hit the buy button three or four times. You've even had your credit card out twice. You agonize over the decision, because you want to do it, you think it will help, but still something just doesn't feel right.

What would it feel like if you *just knew* that was the perfect next step for you? What if you felt like you were led to the right people and opportunities, the ones that are truly perfect and exactly what you need to move forward? What if it was akin to putting an address in your GPS and you knew all you had to do afterward was allow yourself to be led to a business you want to be running?

When your destination, your vision, is complete and solid and you know what it feels like to experience it, you will be led to the next right choice, or the exact person you need to learn from, or work with in support of your vision. You will know when to send out emails that speak to the soul of your audience. You will know what to say. You will know how to market your business in a way that feels really good, and when you do it will even feel easy. You will experience your perfect clients just by showing up.

Jill, one of my clients had that exact experience the night after she finished her vision. She, in her words had been "struggling to figure out how to sell a program (she) had created." She was frustrated and had actually thought about quitting her business altogether. The night after we completed her vision, she was inspired to send out an email about the program. The words were easy to write because she was tapped into her future self, and she sold six spots in 24 hours. She then went on to sell out that program over the next 9 days. Click here http://www.liveyourchampagne life.com/marketing-tool-kit/ to hear Jill tell the story in her own words.

Jessica realized, when we dove really deep into her vision, that what she thought she wanted and had been trying to create in her business *wasn't* what she wanted at all. She actually wanted to be creating a skin care business instead of a full-time coaching business. She wasn't clear, and she was trying to go down a path she didn't really want, which explains why it was a struggle.

I see this happen so many times in business. Entrepreneurs don't give themselves the space and permission to ask their soul what they really want to be doing. They do what they *think* they should do or what they *think* will work and they meet dead end after dead end taking that road. In Jessica's case, once she let herself open up to what she really wanted, she created the complete vision of what that looks like, and her business doubled in the next ten days. Click here to listen to Jessica's story http://www.liveyourchampagnelife. com/marketing-tool-kit/

That is what happens when your vision is clear. You are led to the next step, like Jill was inspired toward sending out the email with exactly the right words. There is no GPS system to put your dream vision in and no computer lady waiting in the wings to navigate you straight to it. The next best thing is to create the vision you want to be living and allow yourself to be guided. That guidance looks and feels like an idea just popping into your head. It feels like words just flowing off the page. It can mean the perfect person reaching out to you to support your next step. It can me, like in my case, being drawn to write a book, or set of books, with a certain publisher.

The results look like selling out a program you previously were having trouble selling. Or making 10 times the money you made for the month of November of last year, in just the first three days of the month. Or doubling your income in the last 10 days of the month. Getting to be a featured author and have someone else promote you. All these things happen easily when you have the GPS point set to your dream life.

This is in direct contrast to chasing things around you *think* might work. Experiencing frustration because you can't get things to work despite more and greater effort. Keeping the buy button of a program open on your computer for three days because you just can't decide whether this investment is right for you, or if it's a distraction. Or constantly looking for the "magic" and elusive course that is going to make all your business dreams come true.

When you are clear, again crystal clear in vivid detail about your vision, the total life you want to be living, then you can create a marketing plan that is easy and fun and all those things you dreamed your business would be. The clearer you are, the clearer your path will be. Many times when you are clear, the plan starts to write itself.

Clarity leads to flow. Have you ever been in a state of flow? If feels like things just magically happen. You are led to who and what you need to be led to. You are inspired to post certain things, or make certain offers, and they are well received—shared with enthusiasm, met with abundant gratitude, or sell like crazy. You have people just "find" you even though they have no idea how. Clients and money flow in in a way that seems almost too easy.

Meeting my realtor is a great example of watching results come from being in the flow. In fact, with me, Brandon was so in the flow he didn't even need to market. He and I met at an open house down the street from where I was living at the time. I wasn't planning or buying any time soon, and I had a realtor I worked with in the past, and someone who would be my first call. At the time, I just wanted to see the inside of these condos that had been built inside the shell of an old church. I would walk by this creation all the time, and I was dying to see the inside, so when there was an open house, well, I went.

Brandon had just released his 9–5 job to do real estate full time, and he had spent some time getting really clear about the clients he wanted to work with, one of which was investors (that would be me). He showed me the place. I told him I had a realtor who I normally worked with, but we had a great time talking about real estate. We hugged good-bye at the end of that first conversation, and I thought we might stay in touch as friends, I never thought he would become my realtor.

A few months later, Brandon saw an investment property that made him think of me. His intuition said to send it over, because I might not have seen it, and he thought because I am an investor I should know it was available. He wasn't trying to market or sell. He was just being in the flow, which includes following your intuition. He was inspired to pass it along. He wasn't desperate or needy because he had a clear vision of where he was going. He was just being nice and helpful.

We went to see the property and I tried to buy it, but it didn't work out. In the time since Brandon and I had met, my former realtor had sort of retired, so Brandon became my realtor—*just like that*. In the two years since we met, he has made over $30,000 from properties I have bought and sold. I was attracted to Brandon's energy and service, actually, not his marketing copy. In fact, I have still never been to his website. I knew from talking to Brandon that he had a clear vision of where he was going. It was attractive, energetically and practically speaking. He knows what his dream life looks like and he is moving toward it every day.

Being in the flow is magical. Clients just show up. Offers to do really cool things come out of seemingly nowhere. This happened to me last year, once I got really clear about my dream life. I posted to Facebook about my upcoming Money, Money, Money course. Someone I knew shared it because she likes me, and had taken and liked the course. Someone in her audience saw it, and this someone has tens of thousands of women entrepreneurs in her community and reached out to me about doing a class for them. My vision was clear, so I was very attractive. I was in the flow, just following my instincts, and felt the need to share about the upcoming course. I have taught a class for that group since, and have the opportunity to continue to do so in future partnerships. When you are clear about your vision, you can move onto the next step. Do you want help getting clear? Click here to schedule a time to talk to me. https://cassieparks.acuityscheduling.com/schedule.php?appointmentType=952439

CHAPTER 5

Create Your Marketing Plan

Once you are clear about your destination, you can start working on your plan. When you are in the flow, you will need to do less than you think you do, and *a lot less* than you have been taught.

Your Ideal Client

The first step in marketing is to identify your ideal client. Going forward, I'm going to call the bottom of the "funnel," the *entry point*. This is the first time people start working with you. Often people create their vision of an ideal client from this point. They imagine their ideal client as the one who wants whatever they are offering at the entry point.

A better way to create your ideal client is to dream up the person who is craving the most support from you (your highest end product or service). What does she or he want? Who is the person who wants to travel along with you because they know you can help them? This is the person who has the biggest dream/goal that you can support. This is the person who will be the most invested in you, your development, and your reach.

Once you identify who they are (download a process to help in the tool kit http://www.liveyourchampagnelife.com/marketing-tool-kit/) identify everything about them so that you can start speaking to them. The client who is just going to drop in and try you out for a product or even two is a slightly different need state than the one who is going to hang around for the long term, and yet a much lesser value client to attract, which is why you want to speak to the long term client.

Remember, if you talk to just one person, others will start eavesdropping. By talking to the one who is going stick around, the others will hear you and drop in for a product or a course. If you just talk to the ones who *aren't* going to stick around, it's not as deep an engagement, and it has less magnetism. You could find the ones who would stick around might not hear you.

Again, if you are clear on the life you want to be living, this will be easy. If it's not easy, go back to step one and get even clearer about the life you want to be living.

Things to Market aka Ways to Make Money

Now that you are clear on your vision, and who your ideal client is it is time to list out all the ways you can think of to make money. List out everything you have ever thought of, every product, service, idea. Get them out of your head and onto paper so you can see them. Look over the list and see if any of them fit together, like stairs that lead to a higher and higher level. Group those together. We will refer to those as categories. Look over the list. What feels like it's calling to you from the page? Highlight those. There is a reason they hold that little sparkle, because they have truth.

Like we talked about, most people with a servant's heart have more than one gift, which is the reality that makes you want to offer so many things. In order for marketing to be super easy, you want to pick one thing or one category. Believe me, I understand the angst that might have just come over you as you read that sentence. It was the same thing I felt when my mentor told me I had to pick *one*.

I had more than three categories of things I was really good at, like teaching people how to love themselves, loa money coaching and loa coaching in general, and then I was going to add loa coaching for sports in there. I pulled up the email I had sent my mentor that prompted the conversation and knowing what I know now, looking at that made my head spin. You can absolutely do everything you want all at once. Or, like my mentor told me, you can do one of them at a time and you'll be more successful, much quicker. My vision was clear and so the decision was easy.

My mentor was right. I first chose being a loa money coach, because that path felt right at the moment. I wanted to focus on getting people into the Money, Money, Money course. And that's what I started doing. I put my attention and energy into making that successful. The course was soon oversubscribed every month, and when I just offered it for the final time, it had 222 people registered.

If I had tried to do everything I could have to make money, all at once, I think I would have only gotten about 100 people into the one course for the whole year. My focus would have been split, and not just between multiple products, but multiple areas of focus. I wouldn't have come to be known as a money coach because my offerings would have been all over the map.

Picking what you want to focus on doing, and who you want to become, can feel like you are cutting yourself off from things you love. In writing, there is an expression about "killing your darlings" that rings true in creating business offerings, too. There will be things you love that you cannot develop in order to create focus and initial success. At first, giving up teaching people about loving themselves felt like I was saying no to something. What I realize now is that I was saying *yes* to lots more things, just in a different order, and fueled by a different circumstance. I've learned that if you structure your business for ongoing support, you get to do everything you love.

For example, when one of my year-long participants is going through a transition period and everything feels like it's falling apart, I get to teach self-love. I get to remind her to be easy on herself. I get to remind her to take extra good care of herself. In certain moments, I get to walk her through forgiving herself and letting go of self-doubt. I get to help her be more confident. I get to teach self-love like I wanted, it's just in a different way, and as a different element of my offering. Remember, one of my year-long participants is one of my most invested, ideal clients.

There are two reasons people don't pick, or allow themselves to focus on one thing. The first is that they're afraid they have to give something up. I'm here to tell you that you *can* do everything you want, it's just that you get to do everything you want in a format that you cannot envision just yet. The second misjudgment is they think that doing more things will make more money. If you want to do all things, that is awesome. Find someone who is doing that and follow them. That person *isn't me*. I could never figure out how to make all the things I was offering successful at one time. That does not mean it can't be done. It just means I can't do it, and it was not the right path for me and I listened.

Over the last year, I have hung out with and been connected to more people making multiple six figure incomes than ever before. What I realized is they all focus on one thing—*their thing*. They offer deeper levels of service for that one thing, and they are rocking their businesses and their incomes. I currently have a $500,000+ business plan for 2016 and I have three things to offer that all fit in the same category. You don't have to do what I do, but in order to make the rest of the plan make sense, I'm going to show you in the following pages will work better if you pick one thing or area of offering to focus on.

Circling back to being clear, the decision to focus on one thing felt a little painful at first, but it really felt easy on the other hand, because my vision was clear. If it feels hard to decide what path to choose, go back to work getting clear on your vision. If you want, I can help you with that. It will be fun, and feel a lot better than spinning your wheels. Click here to schedule a time to talk to me: https://cassieparks.acuityscheduling.com/schedule.php?appointmentType=952439

Once you have a clear vision about where you are going, putting your marketing plan into place is easy. Now that you are clear on what you are going to be doing, and you have eliminated things that don't feel good from your marketing list, let's create the plan.

Here's the secret, pick one to three things from the marketing list that you love the idea of doing, and you think you can do really well. Yes, you read it correctly, just one to three. That really is all you need, when you focus on optimizing what works.

Why one to three things? Narrowing your focus to one to three things is going to give you the time and energy to do them well. If you are doing them well, they will work well, and if they are working well that is all you need. All marketing works.

You *think*, and have probably been taught, you are going to do better if you market your business every way there possibly is to market it. Check all the boxes, be as complete as possible. When you don't have enough sales, the answer is usually to develop a new way to market. Adding a new way to market, if you are still trying to do all the other ways you were previously doing, actually dilutes your marketing and makes it less effective all across the board, because all of your energy is divided.

Before you create your marketing plan, pick the *one thing* you are going to be marketing. Yes, one thing. Pick one thing that you love and you want to be known for. Or the one thing that is working and you wish to optimize.

It's going to be easier for a couple of reasons. Number one is you can figure out if that thing is going to sell at all, and how. Number two, it is going to be easier to track your results. You don't have to be doing a million different things at once. In fact, based on my experience, you will be more successful with fewer things to offer, and fewer activities to manage at any given time.

In traditional marketing funnels, you might have a $7 product and a $27 and $97, then $197, then $497 and then $1997. I never understood this. I mean I get the basis, but I could never figure out how to implement it in my business.

So, I created a whole bunch of products at different prices, because I thought that was the point.

The real point is to keep someone engaged with you and continue working with you. To me that felt like selling, and to a servant's heart that can feel yucky. Some people think you have to hold back in your $7 product because you want them to eventually buy the $1997 product. You don't have to hold anything back. You could give everyone everything you know in the $7 product. They would probably just be overwhelmed if they got 47 hours of video, 300 hundred hours of audio and 1000 worksheets for $7. That isn't effective.

The servant's heart wants to serve. I have found the best way to do that is serve and then keep serving. The question is—and this one, I didn't understand I needed to ask myself when I was creating all kinds of products—do you want to serve their ongoing growth or solve one problem at a time?

Let me explain, you can serve them with multiple products that take one problem at a time and help them out. Or you can help them with one thing, and allow them the opportunity to continue to be served, by you, longer term as they continue to grow.

Here's how my business works. People join my Manifest 10k program because they want to learn about money mindset. Once they start to grow their money mindset, they realize they really want a change of lifestyle and not just more money. In order to serve them, I offer my Script Your Happy Ever After workshop. In this workshop, they get really clear about the life they want to be living and they create and set their GPS point. Once they have created their GPS point some of them want to be served further, so I offer them the opportunity to work with me for a year in a group coaching program so that I can support them staying on course to their GPS point.

My "funnel" is entirely based on service. Remember I talked earlier about how I get to do everything I wanted, by focusing on one thing? I get to be a money coach, because that is where people start with me. Then I get to teach them in depth about LOA at my workshop. Then I get to coach on everything I love in my year-long mentorship. I get to do everything I love, while serving my clients at the highest level possible.

For me, I want to serve at the deepest level possible. This is the easiest path for me to do that. Is it the only way? Of course not. You get to do it however it works best for you. I share my example because it doesn't look just like everyone else's. That is my point.

Ways to Market

Next, refer back to the list of possible ways to market you created at the beginning of this chapter. Add to the list if you need to. Make sure you have them all. Every single strategy and tactic you can think of. Get it all down on paper so you can see it and more importantly, it's out of your head. When you have the marketing possibilities, look over the list you created and make sure that each one you listed is just one activity or channel. For example, if you wrote down "social media" that's really a nest of about 10 items. Facebook, Twitter, Instagram, etc are all single options for marketing. You'll see why this is important later.

After you have reviewed that list, write down every *should* or *have to* thought or admonition you have ever known. Some examples might be, *You have to have a big lists, You should have an amazing website, You have to do high level SEO, You have to be on all forms of social media, You should have a funnel.* The list goes on and on. Write them down so they are out of your head and you can see them.

I will tell you, you don't need to do as many of these things as you think you do. Take your pen and cross off everything that doesn't feel good or intuituitively doesn't feel like it's going to take you to your future vision. If your vision is clear, this will be easy. If it's hard or feels scary, go back and get clear on your vision.

As I mentioned, when I got really clear about my vision, my destination, I started seeing my publisher's name pop up. I saw a Facebook post a friend wrote about her book. And I really felt "called" from the inside to reach out to her. There was no drama in the decision to work with her to write a book as part of my marketing plan. It was an automatic, easy *yes*. When your vision is crystal clear, there really are no decisions anymore. You just "know" what to do.

A few months ago, I felt the need to reactivate my Twitter presence. I have my Twitter linked to my Facebook and I have my tweets scheduled. Some people really hate that tactic, and they have told me so. Others have thanked me for posting what I post and always being there. Always being there requires scheduling, because managing all that presence takes energy.

In the past, if the person who told me they hated the scheduled tweet had told me that, I might have been tempted to change it. She's someone I respect. I let what she said go, because I know this is an operational decision I made in alignment with my goal and dream and that is what is important. The clearer your vision, the less tempted you are to listen to the voices that might get you off track. There are a million different ways to market a business, and none of them are wrong, but most aren't the elements that will take you to living your vision.

One of my year-long clients was struggling, awhile back. She had gotten out of the habit of checking into her vision. I reminded her and she did it. Then she had a brilliant plan to post on Facebook and ask for questions. She asked a few of her friends do it first, to get the ball rolling. That post was inspired from her future self, it was fun and it was effective. It's also a suggestion you might never find in a marketing how-to guide. When she was tapped into her dream vision the ideas started to lead her.

In contrast, what she had done the week before—when she wasn't tapped into her vision—was to post a testimonial from a really well known person which she thought would draw a lot of business. It didn't. Why not? Because it was something she *thought* would work and it didn't come from her vision. It was also graspy and a little desperate. When she posted the question that was inspired and connected to her vision, that post was attractive, not because of the words, but because it came from her future self and the vision of where she is going.

Another one of my clients who got really clear on her vision started posting announcements to Facebook, and then they got shared, and she had a customer right from the first share. Marketing is easy when you are tapped into your dream vision.

Before you move on, make a new fresh list that just includes the ways to market that you did not cross off. Keep only the things that feel really good.

Create a Plan

I'm going to share with you how to market a business plan where you choose to market using just one to three things. Even if you don't want to shift your business plan, you can still learn how to market really well in the following pages. Remember the key to your business and marketing plan is clarity. When you are clear about the life you want to be living the business plan that is best for you essentially picks you.

Now that you are clear on who you are talking to (your ideal client), how you are serving them (what you are selling/ how you are making money), let's think about how these wonderful souls would meet you. You know her (your ideal client) intimately now. Where is she hanging out? What is she looking for? What does she want to hear about? What articles would she love to read? What is going to brighten her day? What does she need to be reminded of? What words is she longing to hear? What does she want to believe she can do? What problem is she trying to solve?

She is amazing, and you have what she is looking for, so how can she meet you? Think of 1–3 ways she can be introduced to you. The three ways my amazing clients can get introduced to me is on Facebook (link to https://www. facebook.com/SpiralUp), Twitter (https://twitter.com/ spiraluptoday) and my Podcast https://itunes.apple.com/ us/podcast/happy-ever-after/id1066349220.

My ideal client can meet me in those spaces, just like when you meet someone new at a party. She can get to know about me through seeing my posts, tweets and listening to my podcast. All you need is one place for people to meet you, and start getting to know you, low stakes. Hang out there often, so they can continue to get to know you, and continue the conversation. Hanging out in 1–3 places and being present there regularly is easier than hanging out in 10 places. In fact I would start with just one place.

Develop a strategy that works *for you* for your people to get to know you. Get really good at meeting people in one place. Make sure it's a place where your one ideal client is reliably hanging out. And if you are meeting a lot of people in one place, focus on that place and optimize it. Make it even better. Give your people lots of opportunities to get to know you so they can really start to like you, and want to meet you outside of that place, potentially.

How do you know if they like you? You offer them a way to get more time with you. If they like you they will give you a way for you to stay in contact with them. In other words you offer them something for free, and they decide if they like you enough to give you their email address so you can keep in touch with them. If they have gotten to know you and like you, they will want to get more of you. This is the equivalent of meeting a new friend at a party. You get to know them just a little bit, maybe for an hour or two, and then if you like hanging out with them, you invite them out for coffee to hang out some more. If they like you, they give you their phone number to stay in contact.

Start with offering one low-stakes, even free, way for people to hang out with you a little more. This could be a checklist that helps them figure something out. It could be a free call where you teach them a skill or a new angle on something. It might be an audio recording or an ebook. There are many possibilities. When you are picking one to start with, think about what your ideal client is looking for. What does she want to know? What would she be so happy to learn from you?

Once they have said yes, they want to know more and they want you to keep in touch with them, make sure you do that. Give them a few emails to make sure they were able to download what you sent them. Ask some follow up questions, and give them a chance to respond.

Then invite them to hang out again, in a more in-depth way, extend the conversation. Offer them the opportunity to keep hanging out with you by offering them the ability to buy something from you. Once they know you and like you, most often they will *want* to buy something from you. Especially when they have come to trust you, or your opinions or advice.

Reminder: When you are clear about your Happy Ever After, this part is supposed to be easy because you know where you're going. You know who you are serving and you know how you want to be serving them.

Now that you know the system, how do you know if it's working? Has anyone invested with you yet? Then it's working. Now, you need to go and optimize the system.

How do you optimize the system? Look at the numbers. How many people had to say they liked you for every one that said they trust you and actually invested with you? In other words, how many people signed up for your free thing, compared to how many people invested with you with a paid product or service? If you had 50 people register for a free call and 1 bought that ratio is 50/1. That means you if you want 4 people to say yes a month, you need 200 to say they like you.

How do you optimize the system? Start with the free call. Did you mention you were going to offer them an opportunity to invest to keep growing? There are so many free calls I did where I forgot to tell them that they could get on the phone with me and talk about how to take what we talked about even further. That wasn't optimized, not even a start. Did you answer the emails you got in response to your follow up questions? That's one way to connect on a deeper level. Did all the links work in the emails? Did the emails actually get opened? These insights can help you make decisions. If they didn't get opened, you can work on your subject lines to make them more attractive and opened more often.

One important thing you want to check into is your energy. Did you do this tapped into your future self? Were you talking to your ideal client? A great way to get the answers with greater ease and clarity is to tap into your future self and ask, "How can I make this better?" Remember the story of Jill sending the email to her list? She was totally tapped into her future self and speaking from that place. She'd sent out *lots* of emails before, none of which produced the results she got when she spoke as her future self. Tapping into your future self and your future vision is the quickest and easiest way to increase your results. (You can hear Jill's story here: http://www.liveyourchampagnelife.com/marketing-tool-kit/)

What if you didn't have anyone invest in themselves by purchasing from you? What should you do? Most people will go get more traffic, they might even buy it believing that is the issue, instead of fixing the underlying sales problem. You have to get a sale before you start going to drive more traffic. Driving more traffic to something that isn't working is like filling a bucket with a hole in it.

Marketing easily does take some degree of patience to test and get it right. It gets easy when you get the formula down. Getting the formula down can take a little bit of time and patience. The more focus you put on getting it right in the front, the better it will be.

Once you know the system works well, you can invest in more traffic if you desire to speed up the process, or amplify the results. But investing in traffic to a system that isn't working yet won't make it work. It will just be a more expensive frustration. If you have already done this you are not alone. I spent thousands of dollars doing this. If you've done it, add it to your list of things to forgive yourself for. It's ok, now you know and now you can do it differently.

Something else to look at as you analyze your system is, "Are you solving their problem?" I have resisted the idea of marketing to the problem for a long time, but something clicked when I heard it in a different way and now I get it. Solving their problem doesn't mean you have to make them feel bad. It *does* mean you have to meet them where they are. I did this the wrong way for a long time.

Loving Yourself University is a site I started four years ago. I was coaching at a conference and a woman came up to me and wanted some coaching. At the time, her marriage was ending, she was losing her job, and I think she was about to file for bankruptcy. It was a rough patch, and she wanted to fix those external parts of her life. I told her, "I can help this all feel better, but nothing is going to change in your life until you start loving yourself."

She looked at me with a look that said, "I have to fix this. I will do anything you say," and then she said, "Ok, but how do I do that?" We started talking about it and I gave her some things to do. In that conversation, I realized there aren't a lot of people teaching people how to love themselves.

There is actually a pretty good reason for that. No one really *wants* to learn how to love themselves. That isn't usually the problem they identify in the early stages of asking for help fixing their lives. Of course *you* have a servant's heart ,and you probably learned along the way how important it is to love yourself, so *you* get it, you know it's important. And you might even seek out a resource to help you do it better.

However, the average person who still needs to learn the value of self-love, let alone how to love themselves, doesn't know that's what they need. They are actually looking for a way to stop having their life fall apart, or figure out why they give so much and get so little in life, or why no one else will love them. They don't know what they don't know. And they don't know that loving themselves is the answer to the problem they are experiencing.

Unfortunately, I didn't know then how to serve "my" client yet, either. I didn't know how to reach her because I was like, "learn how to love yourself" and she was like "I'm crying on the bathroom floor and I don't know what to do." A better name for that site would have been HowDoIStopMyLifeFromFallingApart.com, right? She would have found that site and then I could have taught her the key was to start loving herself, but she never found me because I wasn't talking to her in a way she could hear, at least not yet. That's one more thing I've forgiven myself for. I didn't know what I didn't know. If I had, I would have served a lot more people and made a lot more money during that time. All that is now is experience, and some what-not-to-do stories that help me understand *you*, the new entrepreneur!

The hardest lesson to learn in marketing is how to speak to your client where they are. They don't know what the solution looks like yet. If they did, they would be doing that and they wouldn't need you. Let that sink in. They are seeking the solution to their problem. Almost always they have no idea what solution they should be looking for, so they are seeking someone who understands.

The clearer the picture got about the vision of my life I was moving toward, the easier that concept became. I started to see what my clients needed vs. what I wanted to give them. There's an energetic reason for that. I was being led and guided about how to do things by that time, rather than pushing to make my business work.

The more in touch with your future self you are, the more in the present you are, the more effective your energy for attracting opportunities to serve, and when you have those opportunities, you also actually serve much more effectively. I thought I was serving with Loving Yourself University, but I wasn't. It wasn't my fault. I get it you want to serve them, not make them feel worse, or elude them because you are standing on the platform of the elusive solution. Serving from a place where they can hear you is serving them in the greatest way possible.

Once you know you are speaking the language of your ideal client, and they are making the choice to invest in themselves by buying from you, you can start finding ways to invite more people to get to know you, so they can start liking you.

In all stages of the process you want to track your results. Why? First, you want to know what is working so you can do more of that. Second, it's easy to think things aren't working when you don't know that they actually are. Often, results come in unexpected ways. What you believe about the process matters while in the process. If you believe something isn't working, it's not going to work. Give yourself the gift of knowing what is working and what you can improve on.

The first thing to track, is how people are hearing about you. That's a simple thing to track. Just add a box to your sign-up forms. Most people will tell you. You might be surprised to find out that people are finding out about you in ways you aren't aware of. There might be something you are doing really well, and you don't know it. Meanwhile, you're trying all these other ways to introduce yourself to people. You might also learn that your ideal clients come from one specific source. Again, you'll want to show up there more frequently or visibly.

Then you want to check all the steps in between and see what is working so you can make it better—and if something isn't working you can check into your future self and get the guidance you need to make improvements that speak to your actual, ideal client.

Everything I said above is awesome, and it is the best way I have found to have the most successful business possible. However, the best marketing plan ever is to serve your clients to the best of your ability. Serving your clients, by helping them get the results they desire, will make them want to tell everyone about you.

The Best Part of Your Marketing Plan

Referrals are the best marketing plan. Referrals get to know and like you from someone they already know, like and trust. This is the reason to keep your marketing plan as simple as possible. The simpler your marketing plan is, the more time you have to serve your current clients. That service is what will make all the difference in your clients' lives and your own life, because your business will be much more successful with people referring people to you.

Start Serving Your Clients

The best way to make your marketing plan effective is to first create a super clear vision of the future you want to be living that you can tap into. Then start putting it into out there to serve your clients (sell). If you don't have something yet, or you don't have something that you love, or that fits neatly into your Happy Ever Vision, check into your vision and ask your future self how you are serving your clients. To support the answer coming in easy, stay connected to your future self and your ideal client. Allow the answer to come. It might sound or look different then you think.

Now, put it out there. Instead of going to work creating it, make an offer. Offer it to your current list. Talk about it on your social media avenue of choice. See if you can sell it first. Offer it to the first five people who reserve their spots at half off. See if it sells. If it doesn't sell, it might not be the right thing, or you might not be speaking to your ideal client. Look at your words and decide if you want to try it again in a different way, or evaluate if it's not the right thing to serve your ideal client. Check back in with your future self for guidance.

Selling it first makes marketing easy, because you know it will sell. If it is relatively easy and feels good, then you know it's in alignment with your vision. If you create all of it and spend hundreds of hours on it—like I did with Loving Yourself University—and it's not the right thing to sell, no amount of marketing will fix that. You will end up tired and frustrated. However, if you know it will sell it first, the marketing gets easier.

This feels counterintuitive. It seems like you need something to sell it. But you don't. You can know what you're going to do, for example six weeks of calls with worksheets, but all that production doesn't have to be complete before you sell it for the first time—even sell it out entirely! You are selling the result, the answer to the problem your ideal client has been trying to solve. They don't care about everything that comes with the program. They care about getting the solution they are longing to experience. If they think you'll give them that, they will pay for it up front. They don't need to try it before they buy. They are comfortable buying the experience.

You can sell from a blog post, so you don't have to have a fancy sales page. It's awesome if you want to optimize and build a sales page once you've sold your program, coaching packages, etc. But you don't need it to *start* selling it. You don't need a perfect website. You don't need anything, but knowledge of what you are going to offer and a clear vision of the life you are moving toward living.

CHAPTER 6
What Could Go Wrong?

You now know how to create an effective marketing plan. Before you start, I want to highlight a few things that could go wrong in order that this knowledge will help you navigate them ahead of time. The first one is basic: starting without a GPS point, the clear vision of the life you want to be living. Do not skip the first steps in this book. Creating a marketing plan without the clarity of where it's taking you might create an okay, executable plan, it might even make you some money, but it won't get you there the quickest, easiest way possible.

This plan will work if it feels good to you to go about it this way, especially the part about creating it from a place of clarity. The way to make it ineffective is to think you have to do something in the same way, order or shape someone else says you do. Listen to your future self and honor what she has to say. It's easy to think you have to listen to what someone else says because maybe they know more than you do right now, it appears they have a more successful business, or you think they are smarter or more qualified than you. None of that asset or credibility matters if what they are saying is out of alignment with your future self or the marketing plan your future self creates.

Recently, I had a business coach (who wasn't *my* coach) tell me that I needed to have a better website, and I needed to follow a more traditional marketing path. In the 24 hours prior to her saying that to me, I had made over $2,000. In the six days that followed her telling me that, I made another $8,000. Could my website be better? Yes. Is it a requirement for me to serve my clients and make money, *absolutely not.*

This is the biggest trap or fearful place that I used to get sucked into. I thought I had to do everything everyone else said, and that if I didn't, or I skipped one, I would fail. Well I failed trying. I didn't make money in my business because I was trying to make money in my business without a clear plan and while listening to the opinions and expectations of everyone else. It would have been really easy to feel bad about my site, or believe that coach and start trying to fix my site ahead of serving my clients. I learned that the website might be a great project but was absolutely not essential to reaching enough clients to achieve a level of success that was very comfortable for me.

However, I knew two other things, first nothing about your business has to be perfect to serve your clients and get paid. Second, my future self knew that coach's opinion was wrong. At least, it was wrong for me at the time. If you keep listening to other voices, your marketing plan will be ineffective. First, because your plan will fall out of alignment with your vision of Happy Ever After. Second, you will be listening to their voice instead of your future self. Third, you will start mixing up marketing strategies and your plan will lose cohesiveness. Create your plan, and stick to it, adjusting it as needed to optimize it and make it more effective.

I give you permission, right now, once you have created your happy ever after vision that is, to pick one to three ways to market your business—and not do everything under the sun in order to be successful. Give yourself the same permission.

I had two choices when the business coach told me I needed to make improvements to my website. The first was to get distracted by the input and make the improvements, taking time away from my actual marketing plan and serving my actual clients. Or, alternatively, I could rinse and repeat the formula that made me $10,000 in the first 10 days of the month. If your plan is working, you just might want to make the plan better, but there is absolutely no reason to change it. Just like there was no urgency for me to put my business on hold to completely redo my website simply because someone else told me it needed to be done.

As I've said, your energy is the most important component of your marketing plan. If you are acting from desperation, people will feel that. You can follow all the marking scripts and formulas in the world, but if you are giving off that desperate vibe, people will be repelled and you won't sell anything. The best antidote for desperation is having a clear vision. Getting clear on your Happy Ever After vision first creates the energy of attractiveness and leaves desperation in the dust.

Not getting clear in your vision can also lead to doing things you *think* will work. Creating a plan based on what you *think* will work instead of what you *know* will work will create an ineffective plan. Doing something because you *think* it will work is doing something you have *logically* talked yourself into. It might be traditional marketing teaching, or something you heard someone else who you view as successful say out loud, whether intended as advice to you or not (we covered that above).

How do you know if you are doing something you *think* will work? You will find yourself rationalizing it. You will find yourself thinking about it a lot, instead of acting on instinct and inspiration. You might do it because someone else says it works. You might focus on your perceived credibility of the suggestion. All these are symptoms of doing things because you *think* they will work.

Take a second and reflect. Can you think of a time when you did something in your business that you *thought* would work? Maybe you thought about it for a long time. Maybe you agonized over the decision, or made a decision that didn't feel good to act on. You did it because you thought for sure it would work, or you were desperate for it to work. Did it work out the way you wanted? Did it move your business forward? Did it make you money? Whatever the outcome was, did it feel good? If the answers to these questions aren't positive, remember the feeling you had when you *thought* something would work. When you have that feeling in the future, stop and check in with your Happy Ever After vision and your future self.

Now think of something that had an amazing outcome in your business that felt really good. How did you arrive at the decision to do it? What is instinct, and you just said *yes,* or did you feel drawn or led to it from the beginning? Did it feel like the answer was *yes,* like there was no way to say *no*? Did it feel like whatever it was just showed up at the right time? That is what it feels like to *know* something is your best next move. Follow those paths, opportunities and people, you are recognizing them as right for you and that is real.

Creating a plan based on what you *know* will work leads to the most effective marketing plans. When you get an inspired idea, like the my client who asked a question on Facebook to get engagement, or you feel the words just come to you for an email push, like Jill did, you know they will work because they were *inspired.* They are easy to do and feel natural.

Sometimes inspiration takes a little time to flow, so don't get discouraged if it isn't instantaneous. Another thing that could get in your way is feelings of impatience or assuming you have to exert efforts, to do something to move your business along. In those moments, take a deep breath and check back into your Happy Ever After vision and your future self. Wait for inspiration to hit. Creating a plan that is forced instead of inspired will contain that misaligned energy. Everything you put out from a place of second-guessing yourself and applying more effort will feel forced, and have the energy of trying too hard to make something happen.

You want to be the most attractive being possible. Clarity is attractive. Create your marketing plan with a clear vision of the future life you want to be living, start stepping into that life, and watch how the path appears before you.

If putting stuff out there feels forced or hard, it's a sign you need to tap back into your future vision or maybe a suggestion that the vision isn't completely clear. When it's clear you will take action easily. You will know what words to use. What you are offering, what you need for support will just appear.

Something else that could go wrong is that you get off your track. We as human beings can find way to justify just about anything, especially if we are a little scared of the outcome. Some people think that even our own success can be a bit scary. I do not believe there is a fear of success. I instead believe that your brain likes familiarity, and does not know how to create the unknown. So, if you do not have a clear vision of where you are going, your brain will try with all its might, and will probably be successful, to keep you right where you are.

How might this show up? You thinking that you need to constantly change what you are doing to serve your clients or that you need to add more products and services. It might happen that you feel the urge to take on ten new marketing avenues at once. Your brain might help you think that you need to spend time redoing your website, instead of driving people to your website. There are a lot of ways that you can get off course, and lots of rationalizations that can seemingly support your journey off your hot track.

Early last year, I thought I needed to go put everything I had done together in a bundle on Loving Yourself University and sell it for $97. Everything *in my mind* thought this was a great idea. In my heart I still knew it was going off-path. I knew it wasn't really what I needed to be doing, but I justified it.

Luckily, I have a mentor who could see exactly what was happening, and rein me back into my vision. That detour could have taken me back three months, easily, because so much energy would be devoted to figuring out how to craft it. It would have taken twice as long as anything else, too, because it was not in alignment with my future vision, my Happy Ever After.

It is normal to get off track. Life happens and you can get drawn away from your future vision. Then ideas start creeping up that have nothing to do with your future vision. Your future vision is after all new. Stepping into it is going take dedication, and practice, and trial and error. The more you step into it, the more solid it becomes, but in the process you will likely get off track. The trick is to recognize when you are off, and have someone who can help steer you back. This might be a friend, spouse, coach or mentor.

Knowing where I am now, I know that a three-month detour into creating bundles would have ended up costing me at least $50,000. Of course, this has the benefit of actual hindsight, and I can assess the opportunity cost against actual sales made. Sometimes an investment in a coach or a mentor can seem like a lot of money, but the cost of getting off track and not getting to your Happy Ever After quickly and easily is probably a lot higher. If you have someone in your life already, whom you can trust to help you navigate back, awesome. If you do not have anyone like that, investing in a coach or a mentor that can help you in those moments just might be the best investment you ever make.

CHAPTER 7
Your Happy Ever After

My wish for you is that you create the best possible vision of your life, your Happy Ever After, that you can imagine, and you start stepping into that version of yourself immediately. I know that if you do that, the rest of this business alignment becomes easy, and you will get to live inside that vision before you know it. I don't want you to be still struggling trying to figure out your marketing a year from now. I want you to be actively engaged in loving your life and the business you have built.

The first thing you need to do after you finish this book is set aside the time to get really clear about what your Happy Ever After looks like. In my workshop, this takes about three days and that is what I would recommend for you to dedicate to doing this, even if you are doing it on your own. I know it's a lot of time. I get it, you are a busy entrepreneur, it is hard to spare that kind of attention. Yet what I hear over and over from people who take my live workshop is that they cannot believe how much they *didn't know* they wanted. They always think they have a clear vision, and they realize they have never given themselves the time to create the full picture of their Happy Ever After. Give yourself that gift, starting with your time and intention.

Next, give yourself the gift of stepping into your future self. The person living your Happy Ever After is different then the person reading this book. There is some shifting, growing and changing to do. Maybe even some releasing, letting go and forgiving in order to become the person living inside your dream life. Allow yourself the time and space to do that. This is not a three day proposition, but making room in your life for change, for all the personal work and emotions that accompany change, is going to be required in order to become who you need to be to achieve your dream life.

Once you have gotten clear on your Happy Ever After vision and started stepping into the person who is living that life, then start working on your marketing plan. Once you have clarity about your dream life, and are at least beginning to live into that life with some small steps and time, it is going to be easier than you can imagine. You can do this.

Give yourself a year to grow into the person in your vision. Give yourself a year to grow into the entrepreneur you want to become. This is not a small undertaking, it is a personal transformation process. It's worth it, but it takes time to evolve and come together. When you commit to getting clear, stepping into your future self, and allowing yourself the time and space to follow the path that appears, you can create your Happy Ever After.

How do I know? A little over a year ago, I set the intention to make $500,000 from my bed and my balcony. I wrote it on the inside of my meditation space. At the time I had no idea how I would make that happen. When I asked my inner guidance where I was going, the answer I heard was $500,000. I said by the end of this year, I wanted to be on the path to that.

Before I ever went to work trying to figure out *how* I was going to do it, I went to work getting clear about *who I would be* when I was making that much money, and then what my life would look and feel like. When I had that level of clarity, I started shifting what I could in my current life to look more like my future dream life.

The clearer I became about my future experience, and the more I mirrored my current life to that of my future dream life, the more I was led and inspired to follow cues to who I needed next, the next idea, the next step, the next best way to better my marketing.

Clarity is Queen when you are designing a marketing plan for a business and life you love to live. Clarity is what drives ideas and keeps you on track when a distraction presents itself—and they will. It's the clarity that you have in your future self that lets you know instinctively if something is right for you or if it's another shiny object.

Clarity about your dream life is your GPS point. As long as you stay connected to that GPS point, you will continue to be guided to the next turn, next idea, next right move. And most importantly the stronger your connection is to your vision, the easier your marketing plan and all its practical steps will become.

The foundation of your marketing plan is the attractiveness of your energy. The more attractive your energy is, the more naturally and easily the people who have been waiting for you will find you. The connection to your future vision provides the GPS point and corresponding magnetism to make marketing feel easy and effortless. You know everything you need to know to put your rock star marketing plan in action. Hopefully, you've even started already, before you finished this book. *You can do this.* Someone is out there waiting for you to do this. They are waiting to find you, and waiting to follow you.

Know that no one knows your unique genius better than you do, so they do not have your answers. No one is better at that thing you do. It is time for you to let yourself shine and be seen. The way to begin is to have an inspired marketing plan and the foundation to that marketing plan is a deep connection to your future life. Once you have a GPS point, all you have to do is stay connected to it. Keep refreshing it. Be open to the feedback you receive. When you achieve your GPS point, set a new one. *You can do this.* Once you are totally clear about where you're headed and the life you want to be living, it's going to be so much easier than you think.

When it starts to happen, let it be easy. Don't keep thinking it has to be hard work. It can be easy and you deserve for it to be easy. Allow yourself to tap into your vision, GPS point and be led to the next step, the next idea, inspiration, marketing and money. Allow it to gain momentum and work for you, instead of doggedly working for it.

You know what it's like to do it the hard, frustrating way. So do I—remember, there was a time I didn't have much more than 10 total sales under my belt. I know how to do it the hard way, or at least I know what I was taught and it really felt like the hard way. It was never going to work that way for me. The inspired way is so much easier, quicker, profitable and fun.

Still not sure how to put this into practice? Afraid you're going to mess it up? I get it. I'm not one to read a book and think I can go put everything into play on my own. While you definitely can, sometimes it's easier to engage and learn new behavior with some expert help. Sometimes you want a coach to cheer you on. Sometimes you want someone to confirm you're doing it right. You probably want to get there as quick and easy as possible, right?

If quick and easy is the way you want to go, I'm here for you. In fact, if you're brave enough you can schedule a strategy session by clicking here https://cassieparks.acuityscheduling. com/schedule.php?appointmentType=952439. I'll help you create a vision that sets the GPS point so you can be lead to it.

I want the easy way for you. I want you to experience success beyond your wildest dreams. I want you to feel *good* instead of frustrated. I want you to be confident that you can build and market a business your own way and be super successful.

So does the person waiting on you to serve them. She's out there waiting for you to show her the path, answer the questions she's been struggling in, believe in her until she believes in herself. She wants you to find her. She wants it to be easy for you, because she wants you to have the energy to find and serve her, and others like her, with all your magic.

Dream as big as you can dream. Tap into the experiences you want to have inside that dream. Open yourself up to have everything you ever wanted. Get really clear about how you will experience that life and the path will appear faster than you think.

One of my gifts is giving people the space to open up to their wildest dreams and connect to their future selves. If you want support, I would love to also serve you in that way.

How can I help you create the business and life you love?

About the Author

Cassie Parks loves the ocean, dancing for no reason, and celebrating with champagne, but what she loves most of all is living a life a she loves. She is a best-selling author, international speaker and coach whose passion is leading others to live the life they have been dreaming about.

Cassie retired at 32 by combining her love for real estate and the law of attraction to create financial independence. She believes you can create anything you desire, even that dream you have been too afraid to admit.

Cassie is the host of the popular Happy Every After podcast and the creator of the Money, Money, Money course, which has helped hundreds of people develop a better relationship with money and manifest more money into their lives. Her scripting workshop is one of a kind and allows individuals to discover they get their Happy Ever After and they had the magic to create it all along.

difference press

Difference Press offers entrepreneurs, including life coaches, healers, consultants, and community leaders, a comprehensive solution to get their books written, published, and promoted. A boutique-style alternative to self-publishing, Difference Press boasts a fair and easy-to-understand profit structure, low-priced author copies, and author-friendly contract terms. Its founder, Dr. Angela Lauria, has been bringing to life the literary ventures of hundreds of authors-in-transformation since 1994.

LET'S MAKE A DIFFERENCE WITH YOUR BOOK

You've seen other people make a difference with a book. Now it's your turn. If you are ready to stop watching and start taking massive action, reach out.

"Yes, I'm ready!"

In a market where hundreds of thousands books are published every year and are never heard from again, all participants of The Author Incubator have bestsellers that are actively changing lives and making a difference.

In two years we've created over 134 bestselling books in a row, 90% from first-time authors. We do this by selecting the highest quality and highest potential applicants for our future programs.

Our program doesn't just teach you how to write a book—our team of coaches, developmental editors, copy editors, art directors, and marketing experts incubate you from book idea to published bestseller, ensuring that the book you create can actually make a difference in the world. Then we give you the training you need to use your book to make the difference you want to make in the world, or to create a business out of serving your readers. If you have life-or world-changing ideas or services, a servant's heart, and the willingness to do what it REALLY takes to make a difference in the world with your book, go to http://theauthorincubator.com/apply/ to complete an application for the program today.

OTHER BOOKS BY DIFFERENCE PRESS

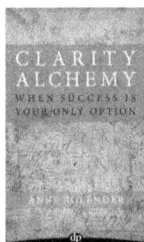

Clarity Alchemy:
When Success Is
Your Only Option

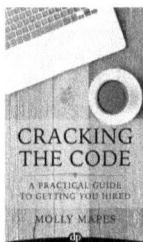

by Ann Bolender

Cracking the Code:
A Practical Guide
to Getting You
Hired

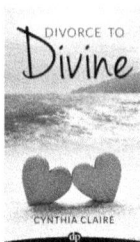

by Molly Mapes

Divorce to Divine:
Becoming the
Fabulous Person
You Were Intended
to Be

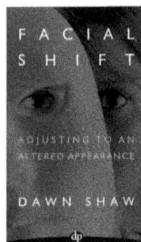

by Cynthia Claire

Facial Shift:
Adjusting to an
Altered Appearance

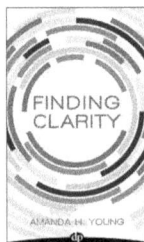

by Dawn Shaw

Finding Clarity:
Design a Business
You Love and
Simplify Your
Marketing

by Amanda H.
Young

Flourish: Have
It All Without
Losing Yourself

by Dr. Rachel Talton

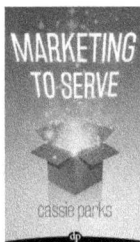

Marketing
To Serve: The
Entrepreneur's
Guide to Marketing
to Your Ideal
Client and Making
Money with Heart
and Authenticity

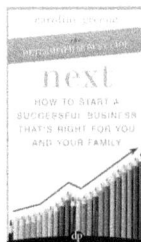

by Cassie Parks

NEXT: How to
Start a Successful
Business That's
Right for You and
Your Family

by Caroline Greene

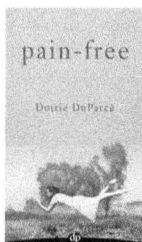

Pain Free: How I Released 43 Years of Chronic Pain

by Dottie DuParcé (Author), John F. Barnes (Foreword)

Secret Bad Girl: A Sexual Trauma Memoir and Resolution Guide

by Rachael Maddox

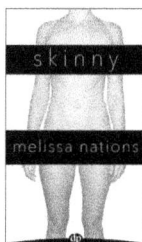

Skinny: The Teen Girl's Guide to Making Choices, Getting the Thin Body You Want, and Having the Confidence You've Always Dreamed Of

by Melissa Nations

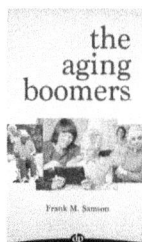

The Aging Boomers: Answers to Critical Questions for You, Your Parents and Loved Ones

by Frank M. Samson

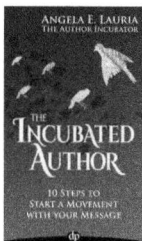

The Incubated Author: 10 Steps to Start a Movement with Your Message

by Angela Lauria

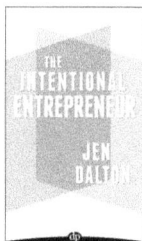

The Intentional Entrepreneur: How to Be a Noisebreaker, Not a Noisemaker

by Jen Dalton (Author), Jeanine Warisse Turner (Foreword)

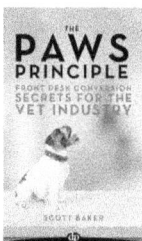

The Paws Principle: Front Desk Conversion Secrets for the Vet Industry

by Scott Baker

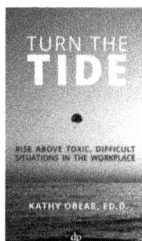

Turn the Tide: Rise Above Toxic, Difficult Situations in the Workplace

by Kathy Obear